Signal / Noise

SIGNAL / NOISE

Poems

Bill Scalia

RESOURCE *Publications* · Eugene, Oregon

SIGNAL / NOISE
Poems

Copyright © 2022 Bill Scalia. All rights reserved. Except for brief quotations in critical publications or reviews, no part of this book may be reproduced in any manner without prior written permission from the publisher. Write: Permissions, Wipf and Stock Publishers, 199 W. 8th Ave., Suite 3, Eugene, OR 97401.

Resource Publications
An Imprint of Wipf and Stock Publishers
199 W. 8th Ave., Suite 3
Eugene, OR 97401

www.wipfandstock.com

PAPERBACK ISBN: 978-1-6667-6037-8
HARDCOVER ISBN: 978-1-6667-6038-5
EBOOK ISBN: 978-1-6667-6039-2

11/07/22

Contents

Acknowledgements | ix

Prelude

    The Last Perfect Day | 1
    Leaves | 2

Part One: Noise

    Noise | 5
    Old Names | 6
    Beat | 8
    Obsidiate | 9
    Green Sprung | 10
    Throwing Off Sparks | 11
    Riff on Ecclesiastes 4 | 12
        I. Synonyms for *Poor*
        II. Synonyms for *Rich*
        III. Consummation of the Flesh
        IV. One Alone
        V. No End to All This People
    At the Mass of Pallas Athena | 15
    Misery | 16
    Split | 17
    Intercession | 18
    Vastation | 20

Fell | 21
    I. The World (So Called)
    II. Fell
    III. The Kill
    IV. Blasted
    V. Just Words
    VI. The Hanging Tree
The People God Kills | 25
The End of Time | 26

Part Two: Signal

More Leaves | 31
Shudder | 32
Mystic Blues | 33
Heart | 34
Goodness | 35
Sing | 36
Mercy on the Road | 37
Adamantine | 39
Transfigure | 40
Sackcloth | 41
Equipmental Words | 42
Is | 45
Here | 46
Signal | 47

Part Three: Return

    Dawn, Day 1 | 51
    When God Called Adam from the Dirt | 52
    Poem of Farmerville, Louisiana | 54
        I: 1967
        II: Everywhere Dogs
    Rough Country Sonnet | 60
    The Revival | 61
    Immanence and Transcendence | 62
    Sign In Please | 63
    The Night of Brahma | 65
    Falling | 67
    The Trial of Belief | 68
    The Measure of Her Flight | 70
    The Next Sound You Hear | 72
    Memory's Ghost | 74
    Sonnet: To Silence | 75

Acknowledgements

"Poem of Farmerville, Louisiana" initially published, in slightly different form, in *Crossroads: A Southern Culture Annual* (Mercer University Press, 2005)

"Dawn, Day 1"; "When God Called Adam from the Dirt"; "The Revival"; "Intercession"; "Vastation"; "The End of Time" initially published, in slightly different form, in *Puzzles of Faith and Patterns of Doubt: Short Stories and Poems* (Editions Bibliotekos, 2013)

"Immanence and Transcendence"; "Sign In Please": "The Night of Brahma"; "Falling"; "The Trial of Belief"; "The Measure of Her Flight"; "Memory's Ghost"; "Sonnet: To Silence" initially published, in slightly different form, in *Pomona Valley Review* 9 (July 2015)

The Last Perfect Day

Three broad leaves
fell at my door:
faith, hope, love—
fugitives from
chainsawn trees

Leaves

Poem, come to me
curled, underleaf
white—let me see
briefly green and
hidden your chlorophyllic
mysteries—

I don't want to know
why and how leaves
grow, lest I
unknow myself in
the too-strict
false glow of
chemistries

Part I: **Noise**

Noise

Broken glass is whirling in my head
high frequencies gigged up
cut my brain into nine million pieces,
each with its own shrieking voice,

each calling one of the
nine million names of God,
unwelcomed—indecipherable

I wake with the taste of gunmetal and
a hole in the head
a prayer for the dead,
feedbacked, looped, distorted, bled,
bleeding out the nine million names of God—

Old Names

Trees grow from
the inside out,
each leaf a testament,
every uplift
to the sun a
testimony—

blood, pulse my limbs
to the sky, you whom
I cannot not name today,
bend my limbs to
the nourishing dirt

Only the old names
breach sky and dirt—
will you break me
in half, please,

where my absence is
most present? Today I
search my heart and
find you absent—

Drive me into dirt,
dissolve me into air,
Oldest Name—
connect me, meet
me in the middle,
inside out

Beat

Beat me senseless, Prince of Peace!
Take up thy rod and thy staff
and beat my brains out—
blast my blinded eyes,
strike so that your glance severs
frontal lobe rigor.
Overturn my tables, Wonder-Counselor—
blight me, your fig tree,
fruitless shamelessly.
How long will you have to put up with me,
good shepherd? So clip me!
Withdraw my withered hand,
sever the offending member—
for who but you, remember,
can transfigure pain into love?

Break me into suffering—
shock me into love

Obsidiate

Burn my heart,
obsidiate God-Word—
green show the glass world
surface, translucid—

Name a poet priest to show
the depth of
the world's longing
for sacred
green glass

Green Sprung

Green is the color of the soul in repose,
green sprung, unwinding coil of
the green world harrowed, wide and deep—
God in the world, a weed by the wall—

Time holds us each
in the clay pot of a dead man
each a split self, a gathering of clay
God smiles—(kind of)—

Time is a machine lubed with ichor—
the clock does not stop,
the space between ticks
a negation—

And we, mere *we*?
Time's swallow—
human clay impaled
on the spires of creation.

Throwing Off Sparks

Three vulgar birds
flutter in the chapel,
throwing off sparks,
silenced by cathedral airs,
brown, muted,

swirling in the vaulted ceiling,
near the particolored and fragmented
stained-glass head of Jesus,
as if asking a torn curtain
for an answer—

how are we here?
have we lost our way
back to the world,
lost our place to sing?

The communion of strangers
murmurs its secret prayer:
Please don't let them nest!
God forbid one of 'em lays eggs!

A few women, leaving,
stop to glean feathers.

Riff on Ecclesiastes 4

    I. Synonyms for *Poor*

oppressions, the
tears of victims—
dead violence.
more fortunate in death?
better off is the yet unborn!
wicked work, rivalry—
vanity, and a bad business.

    II. Synonyms for *Rich*

A three-ply cord.
Two are better than one—
the other will help the one who falls—
and good wage for their toil.
A three-ply cord.
A poor but wise youth, and
all the living—
A three ply cord.

III. Consummation of Flesh

Give me words for my prayer,
give me words for God—
language is the currency,
the only way to pay for the God
condemned to the public.
Unfold my arms and preserve my flesh,
build my body with words—
Better this—don't stretch me full out,
like a sacrifice—
better this, than vanity.

IV. One Alone

The disembodied voice in my heart
is cold comfort,
the book, a stolid pillow—
the nighttime is as quiet
as the newborn world,
silent in its loneliness—
give me a body,
a heart full of blood,
a voice outside my head—
so that we might be
two together.

V. No End to All This People

And the poor keep coming, in endless,
windblown waves
like unscythed grasses—
the billions, broken,
seeking the sanctity of
the three-ply cord:
world without end,
world without end,
world without—

At the Mass of Pallas Athena

I had been watching birds fluttering in the northwest corner of the church, small and brown, parking lot birds, when I noticed her. I had an oblique view of her in the row in front of me, three people to my right. She was tall and of a stately mien, perfectly put-together. That expression is my mother's. *Put-together*. I always took it to mean that a woman is of exactitude appropriate to her condition, status, class, purpose. This woman was *put-together*, seemingly by an internal, inscrutable purpose of self. I noticed her because it was impossible for me not to.

Her hair was long, sandy-blonde, and fell in a perfect slow wave over her wheat blouse like goats moving on the slopes of Gilead. She seemed less evolved than sculpted, less organic than created, in contract with a Titan craftsman. Her grey-blue eyes were Athena's. Her skin was clear and cool.

I stood aside at the end of the row to let others pass for communion. As she walked by I noticed a Band-Aid on her left hand, around the end of the ring finger. The Olympic perfection I had sensed in her was jarred by the single evidence that she was not, after all, inscrutable, and thus sang my heart. She was elevated in my sight. I knew something authentic, perhaps for the first time, in that communion of strangers.

Misery

Thomas Merton once said that
God built us for joy, not for pleasure.
That's alright for Merton, I suppose,
in Gethsemani, surrounded by Brothers
in love with God—

But God built some people only for misery—
Despair is His most sacred unholy gift—
You have seen them: notice the
homeless woman swaddling on the street, alone—
she had a mother—

Notice veterans, old campaigners scattered
like shrapnel through the streets,
the dying who won't die happily ever after—

Notice the rag of a man walking between lanes of cars
with the sign
ANYTHING HELPS GOD BLESS
(*he himself is the sign*)—

See this person
and see in his eyes how glad he is
that he isn't you.

Split

Self,
announce me!
Split-brained,
self and self,
world and world,
defined by absence,
the gap its own difficult presence—

The distance between self and self
is the difference between the swaying of trees
and the sound of the wind—

Prevenient Word! *Signify!*
Wet leaves slip over the gap, and
we stumble,
misspeaking—

Intercession

I walk a dirt road, and as I walk people begin to fall in behind me. Why, I don't know. The road becomes hilly, small and steep hills, so I have the sensation of rising and falling. More people fall in, and a crowd develops. The hills become steeper. Then, on the tops of the hills, I see telescopes, one on top of each hill, on each side of the road. The telescopes are all pointed in the same direction of the sky, at the same angle. Many miles of road. Hundreds of telescopes.

I come to a final large hill. I climb it, with the crowd behind me. It's a long climb, but as I reach the top, the hill flattens into a field of long grasses, swaying gently, the breeze moving the ground like waves. Now it's beautiful, the sun is shining, and I feel good and happy, like I have a purpose, though I don't know what it is.

Inspired, I direct people to tasks. "Bring lumber," I order one group, and though I don't specify dimensions, they seem to know. "We'll put the large post here," I call, pointing to a specific spot. "Then we'll affix the cross beam." I watch a group of people dig a hole for the post, and visualize the structure. I'm building a cross. I'm heading up a crucifixion.

Just then, at the height of my labor, I notice a small cloud, up and to my right. The cloud wasn't there, and then just *was*; it simply appeared from nowhere and originated in exactly in the place the telescopes were pointing. The cloud moves, slowly at first, then gains speed and dimension, becoming tubular. It moves across the sky, right to left, cuts toward the ground, but before it reaches the ground it takes another turn and heads for me.

Is that cloud for you? someone asks, and I laugh. I turn to answer but have no answer. When I turn back the cloud is on me, and then around me. I am inside the cloud. Nothing else is there, not the crowd, the field, the cross, nothing, just a soul and a not-me. I'm boiling hot and my eyes won't close. A face appears *in* the cloud, *of* the cloud, a face I can't describe, with the attributes of something I recognize as a face, but without specific features. It has the faceness of a face without the face.

And then it speaks. I can't hear it. The voice has the soundness of a voice, but without the sound, and it says: *In half your life, you have not done enough for me.* I can't move, or close my eyes, or tune out the voice. Then my vision is obscured. I haven't closed my eyes, but I'm blinded, and I can only see words written in the air, in the cloud. The words are the same.

In half your life, you have not done enough for me.

Vastation

Soft in the velvet void of sleep
a great, white light opens before me.
The light pulls me forward in three slow waves.
I feel the comfort of the light, and then I am inside the light;
my mind contracting and convulsing, pulsing in the depths
    between compaction and expansion,
and I awake, *knowing*.

In the design of the universe, meaning lives in the house
    of mystery.
Three times I tried to wrap the vastation in words, and
three times it slipped away, like a shade, to the underworld.

Fell

I. The World (So Called)

I was born in a house
with air I couldn't breathe,
with food I couldn't eat,
with words I couldn't understand,
a voice I couldn't see.
A strange, alien house—it wasn't
built for me, nor my parents, nor their parents.
But I got used to it—
really, it was very nice—quiet, peaceful.
But somehow—I never really knew why—
I fell out of that house,
into the world
> (*so-called:*
> *God expressed in space is the universe;*
> *God expressed in time is death*)—

but I wasn't alone,
and for this I rejoiced and was glad.

II. Fell

When I fell I fell slowly,
hollow, floated down, emptied out—
What do I recall?
I was running along a green scarfed
road, new-knowing,
and I was tripped by God—
Tell me: how is this fortunate?
Like an empty paint can
dropped from a tall ladder
I made a lot of noise when I hit bottom—
when I awoke, I saw
a shower of emptied cans—
hitting bottom of a hard world,
resistant to our toil—

III. The Kill

It was dark when we fell,
bottoming the world anew.
Did we fall from light?
I don't know—I wasn't there,
and neither were you.
Or, did we
turn off the light
on what we once knew
in that strange, alien house?
Who played this trick on us

and called it *fortune*?
Was God hunting in a baited field?
Like any hunter who baits a field,
the kill must be dragged out
under cover of darkness.

    IV. Blasted

One tree stands
in the blasted road,
its leaves shake
like a serpent's kiss—

outcast to outcast,
the tree of life
is more like an idea of a tree
than a tree—

and all ideas are immortal
until they die

    V. Just Words

And so the road stumbles before us,
a great muddy river that
changes constantly beneath the surface—
the little soul-boat disintegrates,
(ask Thomas Cole!)
our words bounce off the

surface, refract in limpid coils—
a single voice coils
into words
disinterred from reason
with a whip-crack,
transparent
at the edge of linguistic encasement
clear *snap* and
a sound breaks free:
unfit for the text of the river—
this is home,
this boat—
this dangerous river—
this cruel, dark world—

VI. The Hanging Tree

And so we stumble, striving to reclaim the green road,
a translucid poem in hieroglyphs—
and in the final wailing of our
rattle bucket dissonance,
the road impels us—
shot full of holes, blood filling our boots—
to the roots of
the hanging tree.
And for this we rejoice and are glad.

The People God Kills

Saul hath slain his thousands
and David his ten thousands!

Hear my voice, people!
Creation, listen to my song!

Satan killed 10 people in the Old Testament;
God killed nearly 3 million.

They couldn't *all* be stumps of Jesse,
but they were stumps of *some*body.

All of us, denuded stumps—
All of creation, amputated!

Maybe God has more enemies than Satan—
Maybe Satan has more friends than God.

The End of Time

Time stretches behind me as I drive in the mephitic
    August night.
Wretched heat warps the air,
Asphalt steams, out-gassing, silver-blue in the colossal head
    of the full moon.
I smell the great river from the highway, up past Jackson,
    a pungent muddy, a brown fish smell,
    like creation.

In north Mississippi, south of Memphis, I-55 suddenly
    turns violent,
    painted red-black with blood.
Ribs shine white, arched like a whale's, standing above
    a bull's carcass.
The bloating animal spreads an entire lane, midstripe
    to shoulder.

The clock reads 11:11

    I see a man in need, prone on the shoulder of the highway,
        stretched beside his car, and I steer to the side of the road.
    I run down the hot highway's shoulder.
    He rises to meet me.
    I see him in the lights of an oncoming car.
    Then I see fate, like a thick black wave.
    The sound crushes me, and

then all stopped.
The man in the road looks at me still, his bluish-gray eyes
 wide open.
His spine is snapped through his shirt.
His head is cracked open like a raw egg.
His brain lay at my bare feet.

God stopped time, right there in Mississippi, on that night.

God's off hand pulled back the curtain and showed me
 the world behind the world.
Death, the fashioning animus, the skulking machine,
 clean and white, odorless,
timeless,
destroyer of the senses.

This is the way things are, the difference between be and seem.

Then the curtain closed and the stage restructured itself.
Sounds crawled back, slowly, the wind, cars, crickets, frogs.
Palsied, time cranked forward.

Daybreak, on the road, and on the pink-red skin of the sky
The sun puffs up like a blister.
I don't know the time because God changed the dialplate.
Heat burns through the cracks, between time and the world,
 red blazing through a wobbly furnace.
If the proofs were proved and God presented himself,
 nothing would be changed,

and I became hotly aware that all is exact in the mere fact of the world.

The morning heat blurs yellow waves into fired slurry, making focus impossible, and I drive,

longing for return, unknowing, home, hoping that home is still home.

Part II: **Signal**

More Leaves

and words are leaves,
rooted in earth, reaching, always reaching,
through the blithe air,
beyond the sky—
really, does the sky ever end?

Three broad leaves
fall at my door—
faith, hope, love—
the greatest of these
append to the trees
and offer ease
to my vacant heart's hoar

Each primordial word,
itself born in dirt,
appended to a tree,
present, but reaching, always reaching,
through the blithe air,
toward the empty sky—

Shudder

Each leaf sings its condition,
free but attached, till death—
just like words that
point to a surface,
then a sign, a symbol,
then echo and die—
to become mulch
for new words—

Tree are prophets,
arms waving toward
the ineffable veil of darkness,
words falling, dying,
to be reborn
as new words—

Mystic Blues

Ah, the effortless affirmation of religious mystics!
Does mysticism live in the air,
an all-wing, unbodied bird?
Or is it the coffee-talk of angels,
the silent brain-chatter of God?
Does it only live on Parnassus,
or Sinai, or Saturn?
Is Jesus the only one who gets it? Or Buddha,
or Vishnu, or Franklin Roosevelt?

We fire queries at the night,
the canyoned living abyss,
and receive empty echoes—
or toward the pale sun
creeping through the bones of the sky.

Turn your back on air,
these hollow wave forms—
Want to be a mystic?
Ask the weed by the wall.

Heart

Is my heart surrounded by a moat,
a castellated remnant?
or is it a desert yurt?
Is it peripheral,
a peripatos, prolix?
perambulatory?
Is it a shadow that never wavers
in shifting prismatic light?
Is my heart scarred?

O Stella Maris!
My heart is
my heart—
as steadfast as
stars on the windblown sea—

Goodness

What makes an act, any act, *good*?
Is it faith, the disbelieving belief
that routs sense, defies the intellect
with its blinding naiveté?

Or is it hope, the wearying persistence
that your life may not be as terrible as it seems,
that revelation is a process and a destination?

Or is it perhaps charity, which defies experience
and which no one can master?

What makes an act *good* is that God doesn't kill you for it.

Sing

Sing for *her*,
Pharisees,
sing, you goddamned mud!
Sing your seductive song of contracts
and silence her, given up for dead—
Know you nothing?
Well, *she* knows,
at table, afterward—
and she will know
at table in death, fair seeing,
forever feasting of forgiveness—
and Pharisees
have no answer
for that—

Mercy on the Road

This shameful, adulterous woman, right?
She rode the train of mercy like a dancer,
singing one million miles, through the Holy Land
west of Ft Worth,
through Albuquerque, Santa Fe,
to San Francisco
and back before,
to New Orleans, to Babylon,
where the dance began.

In New Orleans flambeaux
set her sacred heart afire;
when she spoke licks of flame
danced around her mouth,
lighting up the dark,
red and unknown.

In the end
she didn't so much die as evaporate—
the fire didn't go out—
it left her clay jar,
extending in a column to heaven,
lighting up the dark night red

so we could see each other by the glow
and dance,
from New Orleans to Babylon
and back before—

Adamantine

Blood
dissolves
rock

Chain links build
their common strength
bound by a lock

Each link in the chain
is God's name
in rusted dust

Keys
make locks
mean freedom

Transfigure

an iron chain
describes the oval
space where
is chains to *be*
as the chain rusts
and becomes
strong

Sackcloth

Poor Jonah—my heart breaks for you—
All you wanted was for God to leave you alone, but
God turned a whale into a machine.
And who else has ever been the direct object of the verb *vomit*?

But you had a shade tree for a while,
and the Ninevites did repent, even
dressing their animals in sackcloth.
Maybe it wasn't so bad, working for God—

So Jonah, Jonah—
Forget about the worm, forget about the tree—
enjoy the absurd comedy of animals in sackcloth.

Equipmental Words

*In the mother's body man knows the universe;
in birth he forgets it.* —Martin Buber

Who said
"Boredom is the perfect state of poetry"?
I don't know—I wasn't paying attention
when I heard the quote.
I was thinking about
Kurt Vonnegut,

as the panel speaker noted the moment
in *Cat's Cradle* when Vonnegut describes the creation,
when God, in his humor, scraped together a pile of mud
and allowed it to speak, and

the woman next to me,
her head scarfed against the cold room,
gives a knowing chuckle.
A finger of light through the blinds dances
one red weave, a constituting pattern,
tracing her outline,

continuing to her young son,
playing on the floor
on his blanket, letters scattered,

tracing his mother's shadow with a
curious finger.

The sighing soul, sloughed off, is
the unnamed absent presence
that haunts its own house.
Boredom is also a haunting,
a haunted reversal, in which
nature interprets *you*.

The haunting of words in the always already world,
a red thread in the world's fabric,
that becomes one thread
constituent of the fabric,
the red current, recurrent, currency,
the word pulsing the current.

When Vonnegut's speaking mud came into awareness,
he asked God, who am I? where am I?
And God gave him equipmental words,
the names of things.

The speaking mud asked God,
    What is the purpose of all this?
To which God replied,
    Must everything have a purpose?
The speaking mud said,
    well . . . *yes*.

God then said to the speaking mud,
    I'll leave that for you to figure out.

The speaking mud gave
equipmental names to things.
One day a speaking mud-thing made a remarkable statement:

    In the beginning was the Word

and the speaking mud had a name for the ghost,
and the ghost had a name for the haunting,
and the haunting had a home,
and *home* was not only a word,
and the mind was smooth,
and the fabric whole,
and we, speaking

the sinewing red line unsayable
just outside the horizon
waiting at the edge
of a mother's shadow

Is

between hemispheres
among lobes
the amplified *is*
in a room of windows,
the lonely verb seeks
a mate beyond the
shimmering glass

Here

is it here?
is it he
re
is he
re here
it is
he
here
it is
is it?

Signal

a clear, bell-like tone
reverberated, dark, deep, wet
the mind is crystal

acoustically transparent
spiritually translucent
humanly translucid

one note somehow sounds
the unspoken speaking
of one unnamable name

Part III: **Return**

An Elegy for the Idea of Home

Dawn, Day 1

Three broad leaves
fall at my door:
Faith, Hope, Love—
but the greatest of these
is the communion of trees

When God Called Adam from the Dirt

When God called Adam from the dirt
He made ribs from catfish bones
He made the heart from *sac au lait*
He made brains from mossy mud and
He made Eve from just the same
He drew her from the fertile soil
He gave her life with steaming air
Like dew from magnolia blossoms—

When Adam heard the sound of the Lord walking in the world
He knew the silence of his mind.
He saw Eve new in his affection.
He saw the land live in the measure of his sight.
He saw children, and he saw a mother,
And he heard their melodic voices on the hot wind.

When God expelled Adam and Eve,
They went downriver.
They rafted to the lower Mississippi.
They settled in the river delta.
They found their work-land, and they were home.

Adam farmed and fished and sweated.
Eve worked the garden and tended the animals.
Able was murdered in the fields.
Cain left home, running from the law.

Their descendants live on in deep Louisiana.
You know them by their muddy hue and their poverty,
By their brown eyes and mossy hair,
And by their desperate laughter, like music on the hot wind.

Poem of Farmerville, Louisiana

I: 1967

The white house hunkered on a red clay hill,
    growing straight out of the ground,
    small enough for one old woman, my great-grandmother and myself,
    a young boy, to spend Louisiana summers alone together.
Mammy and I would get rides to town from one of the Stuarts down the road,
    or go with Pearl or Carene or another of Mammy's party-line confidants
    to Taylor's Market for meat, or to the Farmer's Market,
    or to D'arbonne Grocery for Fresca, Chocolate Soldiers, Jell-O, and other essentials.
Five miles from town we passed time, surrounded by heat
    and the yard that separated us from the woods.

Mornings, I gathered eggs.
I reached in the upper row of nests, just above my head.
I can still feel the hair on my neck spike as I try not to think
    of the chicken snake that may be there.
The eggs, beige and smooth, still carried the hen's warmth.

Days, I climbed the pines and cedars close to the house, but
    not so far away as to be swallowed by the woods,
    or carved my name in the hardpan with a stick, or just
    wandered the dirt roads that led nowhere to my sight,
    like a pilgrim going nowhither.
I was never bothered that we didn't go anywhere,
    or that Mammy couldn't drive,
    or that she'd never had a car, or that the house
    wasn't air-conditioned.
I never knew how poor Mammy was, or my parents were,
    when they grew up
    in Farmerville in the 1940s.
But I did know the fun of dirt I could dig in that changed color
    from sand to light brown
    to dark brown, to red and then almost purple the further
    down I dug,
    and the wet clay that told me I couldn't go any deeper
    on my own.

My only enemies in Farmerville were wasps,
    brown just shy of burgundy, with anvil heads and armed tails.
In hot rooms, windows always open,
    wasps swooped in through holes in the screens.
Mammy would swat them with a rolled-up *Farmerville Gazette*,
    find where they fell, and cut them in half with a scissors.
Half-wasps littered the window sills and baseboards.
I gloated. I figured them acceptable losses in the holy war
    of wasps and kids.

Some very few times I would sneak into the labyrinthine
 "bird room,"
 the door held closed by a screwdriver through a rusty hasp.
I would creep in and look at the birds, hundreds of them,
 porcelain, glass, plastic, finely folded paper birds and
 rough pictures of birds,
 and tangential images of Mary and Jesus.
Scattered among the established slough were pieces of my father's
 compact childhood:
 a pen-knife, a tiny plastic B-29, a rusted soldier, relics from
 the sepia 1940s.
The room was fundamentally musty and always held firm to
 the side of the house.
No one ever purposefully went into the bird room.

Most afternoons Mammy joined me on the porch, and we drank
 bottled Coca-Cola,
 cold from the icebox, and played chicken-foot dominoes and
 waved at every truck that passed, whether we knew it or not.
She kept score, and after every game she'd ask, "you ready
 fer something t'eat?"
 her voice like fried chicken and syrupy iced tea.
And eat we did, anything we could fry up, and peanut brittle too,
 teeth-breaking hard.
Some nights we watched television.
I recall black and white ghost-images of Porter Wagoner &
 Dolly Parton,
 Lawrence Welk, and Granny Clampett.

We slept on the floor, pulling the mattress off the big bed
   in Anne's room.
Anne's room was always closed, like the bird room.
Anne had come to stay ages ago, sick, and she died in that room,
   in that bed,
     years before my father was born. I never learned her relation.
Sometimes, just before sleep, Mammy took out her false teeth,
     held them with ventriloquist skill, and chomped at me
     as I was dwindling away.
We laid on the cotton tick mattress on the back room floor.
Under the tin roof, box fan humming in the window,
     tree frogs, crickets, and owls rang an august performance.
When cool rain sprayed through the screen in a fine mist
   over me
     I thought it was what paradise must be like.

Thirty years later Mammy, 100 years old, lived at D'arbonne Hills
   Nursing Home,
     and I lived in the house alone.
One night in February, after an ice storm, electricity gone,
     the deep black night stood contrast to a colossal silver
     full moon an hour after rising.
I watched through the branches of the Nordic, leafless oak
   in the front yard.
Then I shifted focus:
     I saw every limb and fragment of that oak coated
     with thick ice.
The moonlight made them all luminescent, like a tree that was
   burning,
     but was not consumed.

II: Everywhere Dogs

My other grandmother, Gladys, lived on the other side
    of Farmerville
where houses grew straight out of the woods.
Yards were unbound, and were not yards at all.
Everywhere, dogs—they must've come right out of the clay
    and mold.

The lone but vital well lived behind the kitchen. A gray barrel
    over a deep hole;
    the water drawer looked like a torpedo.
The only bedroom had for a wall a manic belt-driven fan.
There were no locks, or knobs, on any of the doors;
    they pulled closed and latched with leather straps
    and wooden pegs.

Locals dumped garbage in big piles in the woods.
These piles housed great .22 targets, like steel Schlitz cans
    and big Gallo Port wine bottles.
I got dirty and smelled bad. Bathing meant drawing water
    from the well
    and heating it on the stove.
I can't ever remember bathing at that house. The smelly
    romance of the dirt
        catalogued me.

Afternoons were spent at the Lake D'arbonne spillway.
I stared at my reflection in the still lake and dropped in a rock,
    shattering the image. I didn't know about metaphor.
We fished all day and gutted the catch for supper.
The alternative was killing our chickens or rabbits. I was never
    asked to do this.

Gladys watched TV during the day.
She always sat in her naugahyde recliner, a castoff from
    someone "in town."
It must have been brown—everything was—and I remember
    great duct tape patches.
She ate, drank, and smoked, all at the same time,
    her essentials heaped on a set of ugly brown shelves.
She smoked Parliaments and drank Schlitz tall-boys.
She ate anything from pig that wasn't authentic meal work:
    snoots, feets, tails, ears.
Gladys liked to dip the tails and feet in Bama grape jelly,
    a true Farmerville delicacy.

Now Gladys' shelves hold bound books and slick-covered
    snooty journals.
Just beneath the new stain and varnish lie the memories
    of beers and smokes
    and feets and tails.
How far has this bookshelf traveled, now holding
    remembered scraps of
    my cataloged past?
Will I live long enough to get all the details in? Will I die trying?

Rough Country Sonnet

The grayed oak stump at twilight
haloed by jets of setting sun,
disordered, truncated, with its gray rivulets,
stands as its own intention.
A leaking garden hose wreathes the stump,
like a living rope faithfully drooped.

On the flat top of the stump stands a severed potato fork,
its prongs bent over, grasping, rusted.
The claw stands upright, the stump's one hand,
pulling itself from the earth that slowly eats it,
    this Brahma's stump,
its claw the seal and print of rising and reaching.
I see the stump, and correspond:

Refracted through the stump and claw
the mind and machine of nature.

The Revival

As a child I saw a tent preacher
Hammer at his bible
Shouting lamentations and punishments
For we miserable sinners,
Whose feet will slide in due time.

As he defiantly strode the stage,
He smote the open book with his palm, and
Leaves tore from the spine, fluttering to the ground,
Like the wings of falling doves.

These dying wings
Emblems of our failure
Were sadder to me than any implications of torture.

When I got home I looked in my father's bible
And saw the pages intact,
Their wings folded again,
Ready to bear the weight of me.

Immanence and Transcendence

Between immanence and transcendence,
the Seat of Wisdom, sword in hand,
fixes an indefinite gaze.

Her unknowing stone eye is
a rock, kicked,
offering neither refutation nor revelation.

Her head bowed,
she frets one stop on the cosmic monochord,
she and her son sharing their umbilical secret.

The crack of brittle flesh—
the taste of blood in your mouth—
necrosis—
the opposite of sacrament—

Sign In Please

UNNAMED SPECIMENS WILL BE DISPOSED

This sign greets registrants at the doctor's office.
I sign my name and sit amid a timberstand of magazines:
Family Circle, *Highlights for Children*, *Field & Stream*.
Bob Dylan stares blankly from the cover of *Time*.
Jean-Pierre Léaud disguised as Antoine Doniel longs
    from *Cahiers du Cinèma*.
Johannes Kepler and Tycho Brahe figure *Sky & Telescope*.

I don't know her name, or anything about her,
except that she sits across from me in the waiting room,
tall and thin in crisp middle age, in clean workout gear,
holding a plastic bag.

From the bag she takes long slips of identically marked paper,
    blood orange,
dozens of samples, gridded into eight squares,
a different word branded in each square.

She stacks several of them and then cuts the words,
creating a pile of severed language in her lap.
Some of the words fall at my feet:

MORTAR   LOVE   BROKEN   ENGAGEMENT

At intervals she stops her cutting and places a handful of words into small white envelopes.
She seals each envelope and repeats the process.

LOVE   MORTAR   BROKEN   ENGAGEMENT

the words flutter bleeding to the floor
in the clinical sterility of the office.

BROKEN   ENGAGEMENT   LOVE   MORTAR

a signified body without ligature
naming without relation
saying without reference

SPECIMENS   UNNAMED   DISPOSED   WILL BE

The Night of Brahma

Brahma stirs and dissolves the world
shadows dissolve through the skin of the Brahma's dream
and the pieces coalesce as he sleeps again
not in the same order, but
like Bob Dylan canting and recanting, slipping through identity
like Pierre Broca and Karl Wernicke, locating verbs and nouns
    in the whole brain
like Antoine Doniel, staggered by desire, in Truffaut's
    fertile dreaming

The Universe has three children
unnamed, renamed, slipping through identity

superego, ego, id
priest, prophet, king
the knower, the Doer, the Sayer
unnamed, specimens, disposed

Brahma, Vishnu, Shiva
Groucho, Chico, Harpo
Lily, Rosemary, the Jack of Hearts
Faith, Hope, Love

We can no more live without love than we can live without skin.
Love is the skin on the world, the skin through which we move, and
through which we express everything we know, do, and say.

Antoine Doinel lurches beyond the skin of desire, feeling without seeing,
looking through the woman he loves to see the women he desires,
always fluxed by the chaos of being beyond his desire's target.
Johannes Kepler spent his life building a dream of perfect Copernican geometry.
He could not accept retrograde motion or irrational elliptical orbits.
He could not liberate God from the unjust prescription of geometry.
Kepler's dream dissolved, the mathematics leaching from the skin of perfection
broken into the universe bound by the irrational geometry of love.

Falling

Do we show our children God in a blade of grass,
or the universe in a cup of coffee?
The growing trees are tomorrow's forest.

My mother drifts by the willow—
its tendrils reach to her
wrap around her
saying

I will care for you
I will bear you up
I will hold you close
no longer weeping.

I will swing you low, oh my mother,
close to the ground, but not in it,
and I will swing you high, my mother, to heaven,
but not of it.

Swing in my arms,
Swing with me high into lightness and grace,
Swing low, falling, into love—

The Trial of Belief

Fall in love every day, every hour, every minute.
Be homeless in your love;
Logic has no home here—

Live in the falling, in the vertiginous spin
of the ground disappearing beneath your feet,
of the air becoming thin around your head.
Realize the fear and pleasure of participial love,
falling, ever falling, without end, without bottom.

Live your love in the trial of belief.
Faith is being floated; belief is the work of not-drowning.
If faith is air, belief is breathing underwater.
The oracle has said *The urge to believe is stronger than belief itself.*
But I say the urge to believe is enough.

The thymoetean trick of love is to fall and never land.
Therefore be, just be, be just, and then be happy
Be happy like the light that finds the mold on the underside
    of a leaf
Be happy like a discipient Harpo Marx in a crowded room
Be happy like Antoine Doinel in *Baisers Volés*
Be happy like Emerson, glad to the brink of fear
Be happy like the Godhead, broken up, and we are the pieces
Be happy in your brokenness

Be happy like the Brahma in his four billion year sleep

Be happy like the Rabbi, telling the woman in sin that her faith has saved her, and

Be happy like the woman in sin

Be happy like Dylan's simple geometry of flesh on the bone

Be happy like the poet lubricating the muse

> (foolish poet! to not know that the muse is free
> to everyone)

Be happy for Broca and for Wernicke

Be happy for nouns and verbs

Be happy you are not God (what use are verbs to God?)

Be happy with your giant lateralized brain

Be happy with handedness and stereo vision

Be happy in breaking an unjust law

Be happy like Kepler

Be happy like the sun, tracing its analemma in the sky for another 1.5 billion years, and

Be happy that you are not an infinity.

Three broad leaves are
falling at my door—
Faith, Hope, Love
Is the greatest of these
from a single tree?

Be happy that love is not a single tree, for
Love is the communion of the forest

The Measure of Her Flight

At the end of the last perfect day,
in the graying light of her own solar eclipse,
she affixed a rope to an arrow
and shot it into the air.

The arrow stuck in the fading blue and
she climbed to the top of the sky.

She tore a hole in the sky to climb through, and
on the other side of the sky she directed herself
    to a distant moon
within the measure of her flight.

She collapsed toward the dim gray world,
giving herself freely to its gravity, and
soft she landed in the velvet grip of the moon,
forever free of bitter complaint.

She melted into the dense shadow of eternal night and
then, in the superluminous darkness, I knew the dread vision
    of the gods
in their aporetic might.

In the fatalism of a solar eclipse,
    Some people like to see the hieroglyphic stars in the daytime
        as a dragon eats the Sun,
   six minutes of night without the long commitment
        to darkness.

Some look at the corona,
invisibility revealed,
which we cannot see directly lest surely we die. And

Some, vacated,
are left to stare at the blistered hole in the sky.

The Next Sound You Hear

The end is always close,
so the doctor said—
The next sound you hear will be
    the sound of her agony
    her unending chant of pursuit—

The next sound you hear will be
    the sound of her voice in the garden
    outside of your head, outside the comfort
    of your experience—

The next sound you hear will be
    the sound of her dreaming,
    of her stretching time
    beyond its tick-tock (but never *tock-tick*) borders
    to the spaces time can't reach
    and space that doesn't know x and y indices—

The next sound you hear will be
    her dispersing breath—
    Listen closely:

yh / wh   *yh / wh*   *yh / wh*

the next sound you hear,
so the prophet said—
    will be
    the last sound you hear—

the next sound you hear
    makes us free

Memory's Ghost

Now milk-white veils of fog drift in the cold air,
wreathing like ghosts in the trees—

you,
an image, a trace,
a whisper
in my mind
and nowhere
else—

the verb of nature,
a passive voice,
a hole in the sky
from whence comes
cold, rain-stopped lines

and memory's ghost
wreathing the world vacated,
like drifting blue white veils caught in the trees

Sonnet: to Silence

For you, who fires silently in the magazine of love,
and who forever knows the rested quiet night,
quiescently limned, the believer's vibrant rite,
the sound of a snowflake gracing a velvet glove.

And for your cacophonous soul's silent respite,
midnight solemnity escaping from breathless noon—
do you now hear the tolling of the moon,
and know the language of the dove in flight?

We, left back, only hear the whispered "soon"
and know the ever shifting, verbèd sand.
But you are be in the author's verbless land,
and hear forever as mesmer's silent June.

Do not despair over the leaving of your breath;
the silence that you know is not the silence unto death—

Made in United States
Orlando, FL
13 November 2024